In the shadows,

darkness to light

By Peter F Kelly

Other titles available by Mr. Kelly –

In the neural sea

Across the cosmic plane

Singularity reached by

The light of infinity is found

Madness to wrecks

Waiting at the doors

Inspiration of fools

Authors by the scores

The light of infinity

Great promises attached

Cure all, shield, weapon

Host with all you can ask

A living being

Part of cosmic family life

Intelligent power

Sovereign in its realm

2

Riddle of the Sphinx

Question of old

What are you

Little figure of a man

Answer wisely

Proctors are present

Oral exams

Not just test books graded

On placement determined

Classmates and teachers

Schools all similar

Throughout the system

Advanced technology

Psychic schoolhouses

Distance learning

Amply provides

On your shoulders

What do you bear

Organic matter

Lump of clay

Schools disagree

On the specifics

But they all present

A student wide view

On your shoulders

Intelligence looms

Whether brains, or

God's mind at work

How much you know

A matter of degree

Level of education

In your school system

4

Where the mountain side

Of sunny and shady slopes

Where Mount Zion

Or Heaven's gates

Are they found

Outside printed texts

Do they exist

Somewhere in space

Are they imaginary

Only existing in minds

Are they symbolic

Dreams or potentials

Are they realms

Distant dimensions

With different languages

And scientific explanations

In shadows cast

By inner lights

Mind bright

Scenes appear

Mind laboratories

Mind machines

Mind technology

All physics valid courses

Undiscovered

Or unspoken

In public places

Mind developments

Dreams mute evidence

Creation possible

Virtual enclosures

Sensory plane scenes

6

In the shadows

Of balcony seats

In the cavern

Beyond daylight

Trancers' roam

Unlit streets

10

Live in houses

Technology hid in

Dreamweaver's spin

Webs of sensory patterns

In controlled dreams

And magical acts

Life flourishes

On the cavern floors

Filling pockets

With life forms

On the foundation

Of composition's form

A deeper dimension

Appears to some

A realm immeasurable

Of ceiling capacities

Maximum forces

Faire wings

Others a building

Live inside of

Cogs and wheels

Composed structure

The same sights

Shared by both

One written in stone

The other in ice

8

Conviction

Steady application

Regular studies

Knowledge can buy

Experience can teach

Approached right

13

As contemporary

A class in progress

Texts their information

Present the audience

For casual read

Or earnest study

Light's brilliance

Can illuminate or blind

Light the way

Or leave incapacitated

All alone or

In company of invisibles

Appear alike

At a quick glance

Talking to beings

Others cannot see

Invisible companions

Could explain

Madness often called

Those of the sight

Seeing beings or speaking to

Those not seen by others

Talking to strangers

Often warned about

Invisibles behavior

Worth a warning too

10

What hand dealt

In what house

At what table

The cards you play

What shoe from

What deck style

16

What game playing

Receiving your hand

How long a game

What stakes played

What the score

History of the game

How many playing

How large an audience

What degree level

Reached in the game

The common lot

Home to wizards

Grounds of demons

Witchcraft scenes

The average player

Perfectly performs

Full theater span

In range abilities

The audience

Attending everywhere

Merry fellows

Out for a show

Life

Fiction and nonfiction

Entertains many

Is their favorite show

12

Beyond appearances

Public disclosure

What known by you

Of things unseen

Reports alone

Lofty theories

19

Pragmatic sciences

Anything

Transparent or invisibly

Before all review

Inner and external infinity

Exist beyond experience

Now you know something

Perhaps new to you

Beyond appearances

Yet in plain view

Beyond mortal eyes

On eternal shores

Snakes shed lives

As well as skins

Character acts

Played for lifetime lengths

Given curtain calls

Seen never again

Or long running acts

In media production

Cancelled at length

No longer shown

Time is so lengthy

But commitment varies

To personal acts

Even that habit

14

Hold your breath

If you can't for long

Or as long as you want

You're addicted to the stuff

Air, food, body fluids or parts

All can be habitually attached to

To incapacitating levels

In infinite relativity

All products of the mind

Agent operations

Share much in common

Sensitivity, intelligence, etcetera

Chosen habits

Can endow or cost you

Fortunes over time

Given time enough

Bullies and guardians

Co exist on life's stages

In fiction and nonfiction

Like children at play

Future looms overhead

Always older, growing

Reaching ripeness

Growing to juicy fruits

Life the path

As well as result

Knowledge takes

To contributing

A gift of nature

Or husbandry's skills

Everything existing

Along the way

16

Mighty winds blow upon

Little candle lights

To see if true Agni dwells

In such small sights

The founding family of gods

Born of lightning blasts

Like gifts of knowledge

In natural hierarchy

Shady slopes born alone

The sight did not see

The sound reached all

Caring for attendance

The beginning a created sight

An accumulation event

Of contributors works

Expressing their self

Not scary to children

Or innocent pets

Psychic police patrol

Permanent resident guests

The universes law

Easily learned in simplicity

Be correctable in errors

Not permanent mistakes

The panel of experts' rules

Never does it judge

Simply recognizes and corrects

Every act performed

Categorical errors

Terms are made for

Errors too expressed

In language arts

18

The mirror light

Suspended in mind

A new reflection casts

On its carried light

Sights shown glow

Of hidden reservoirs

28

Reflected light signals

In the revealed sight

Fusion potentials

Exist in such mirrors

Generating power

To fuel creations

The light of infinity

Possible to reach

In such surfaces

Reflective power

Natural and true

The Goddess invites

Come to me children

And drink of the light

Her daughters

Liberty and knowledge

And ancient wisdom

Grow minds by their study

Her son power

Wise in judgment

Resident expert place

Holds at the table

The family large

Honeycomb pockets fill

Growing in numbers

Of assets, rich and ill

20

Critics abound

Popular with their crowds

Warnings and green lights

Providing at a glance

Newspapers carry

Critics' reviews

Spreading their views

To the circulation

School monopolies

On criticism

Slanted press

Slanted eyes can make

Healthy criticism

Audiences support

Range of theater cover

In their reports

The world can seem large

Gazed at from inside

Seen from outside in

Everything seems small

Only external infinity

Large proportions possesses

Its sphere the grand oasis

Where dragons dance

Infinity shrinks

Contents to characters

In plain sight

Even masses in light

The all Seeing Eye

Its knowledge obvious

Transforms planets

Galaxies and universes

22

Fleshy feast manifestations

Spirit beings can materialize

Edible body suits with hoods

Even dressing in tasty layers

Playing love games the reason

Dressed for passions undressing

34

Preparing for lovers role play

Dressed to strip for love

Animal spirits delight in these

Shown a transforming light

Warm themselves by the sight

Of spirits in edible layers

Role players the rest

In foodstuff all dressed

Feigning to be the meal

They wear on their backs

Mystery

Initiate role

Drama enactment

New perspective

Life the same

Viewed different

Potentials revealed

Mastery to gain

Beyond phenomena's veil

In the theater of mind

Drama plays out

Mystery initiation

Invisible spirits

Visible images

Juicy fruits

The players

24

Prone, needy

Full of wants and desires

Aspirant approaches deity

Aspirant asks for help

Composed, content

Full of life's good

37

Deity hears aspirant

Deity responds

Life's exploits produce

This scenario again and again

The prone in need

The deity benefactor

Specifics vary

Contexts change

Basic pattern

Remains the same

Deity undercover

Player by trade

Performance vehicle

Born on stage

Interacting with environment

Opening the door to theater

A role is performed onstage

A life story is told to the audience

Establishment a pyramid

Tiers of profit levels

Like monkey bars

In the playground

Climbing to the top

An easy feat

Without fear

With a good grip

26

Friend of God

Knower of the law

Teacher of faith

Priestly titles

Offering prayers

Making sacrifices

Tending the altar

Priestly duties

Rites of passage

Guidance services

Instructional assemblies

Priestly rituals

Spiritual life

With God and gifts

Innocent knowledge

Priestly life

Acquaintance, introduction

Courtship, romance

Two become a couple

Lovers emerge

Winds of fortune

Wheel of fate

Marriage

Or heartache

It's a conflict scene

Protagonist and antagonist

Play in this game

Two opposing teams

Lovers dreaming

Nightmare prone

For the lucky

Good dreams come

28

The living machine

A vision plane

Invisible stealth shadow

Parking mode

Honest relationship

God ship reveals

43

Confession lacking

Environment

Landlord, employer

Police and peers

History and news

Stage setting

Approach, ask

Seek a relationship

Don't give up

Until answered

Average awareness

Level of intelligence

Developed skills

Average character

Limited strength

Vulnerabilities

Necessities

Theater fare

Storyboard

Limited environment

Conflict

Theater tools

Mind power

Mind technology

Mind screen

Mental theater

30

With limited reception

Seeing only a view

Life so much larger

Existing outside you

How old the story

Told to you

46

About life, reality

All you view

Is it as old as the scene

Is it older than time

Does it start

In the beginning

Does it include God

A family treasure

A priceless resource

The ancestral deity

Concentrate

How illusory is experience

Is it only sensory phenomena

Is it a mind construct

Cave dwelling

Seeing shadows

Reflections in mind

Interactive with you

How validated

Mind independence

Separate existence

From mind possessing

How valid a scene

Universe energy signal stream

Without natural transmitter

Without programmer

32

Anything goes

But self destruction

Guardians exist

Psychic police

Liberal government

Jurisdictions support

49

Of lower courts

And principalities

Prohibitions

Protectionism

Monopolies

Hence exist

True self eternal

Unbound, a treasure

All seeing, all wise

All powerful

33

In the balcony seats

Treasures are shared

Spiders dwell content

Secrets are revealed

Looking over the cavern

By radar picture scan

Scale is uncovered

Universe explored

Operating the ham radio

Friends are made

God contacted

Communication begun

In the mind lab

Machines made

Power sources explored

Futures planned

34

Virtual reality

Waking life's scene

Balcony spiders share

In their cave abodes

Virtual interaction

In the cavern universe

52

Enables productivity

Family and social life

Virtual lab work

Provides research area

Explores power sources

Enables mastery attainment

Fossil fuels burning

Addictive dependency

Hysterical delusions

Can infect with

Beyond appearances

Behind the scenes

Psyche dwells

Omnipotent and wise

Invisible inside the cavern

Vaster than the universe

Hinted at in the balconies

The infinite lord creates

In the spider caves

Unbelievers dwell

Living charmed lives

In their dream machines

Believers in caves

Have radio contact

Spirit manifestations

Ancestral deity connections

36

World Theater presents

Survival of the fittest

Predatory examples

Catch, kill, devour

Business preying on labor

Consumers buying spoils

55

Gladiator contests air

Idols are made

Entertainment

The backdrop theme

Of much business

Tickling the audience

Religion a smugglers route

Passage to Godhead

Entrance to mind complex

Path to infinity and beyond

Religious unity

Beneath the presentations

In the message units

Says the same

There's a creator

We are his works

He can bless us

Just come to god

Now in the stupor

Experience interacting

That's incredible

If not unbelievable

A creator real

Life its creation

A spiritual reality

That is news

38

Step into your shoes

In minds eye space

Enter headquarters

In the cosmic order

Prepare yourself

To meet your maker

58

To learn of psychic light

Beyond the visible spectrum

Greet the natural mind

External infinity

Internal infinity powered

Particle scientist

Salute your alter ego

Higher power and guide

Resident expert

Your super self

Like a space mission

You need launch

Your expression vehicle

Into mind theater

You need leave

Gravity and atmosphere

For life support

And vision capsule

Travel in an illusion

Of time and space

Until arrival in mind

Reaching mind space

Mind machines

Mind power

Will mark the way

To the mind complex

40

Beneath Shamballah

Below snow capped peaks

On the valley floor

The glaciers creep

Historic ice flows

Their cold power

61

Hold valley life

In winters grip

Frost bite, hypothermia

Common occurrences

In winters sleep

Without enough heat

Ice giants, snow beasts

Winter games players

Snow bunnies, holly

Winter wonderland rises

In mind space abide

Plant yourself in mind

Nourish on its living light

Bask in its psychic light

Mind streams

Your daily scenes

Mind space

Your environment

Mind games

Played by circles

Like quilting bees

Patchwork blankets make

Mind pieces

Their moves make

Their shots call

Their balls sink

42

Dreamtime includes

Sleeping and waking up

If a dream resumes

Waking life may result

Waking life a dream

A waking dream

64

Daydreaming coherently

Instead of chaotically

In dreams lucid

Order replaces chaos

Control is gained

Consciousness achieved

Sleepwalking

Dream walking

Lucid control

Waking dreams include

Immersed in sea life

Member of singularity school

Family with all beings

God gifted spirits grow

Perfect little mirrors

Reflective of life

Showing their images

To all who see

Knowing light from darkness

Sunny side from shady

Inner light guides them

Through all information

Sharing a law in common

Be perfect as father

They court life's graces

Sharing a social scene

44

Creating new values

Enjoying family life

Monitoring investments

Scenes in faithful life

Forging new languages

Writing programs

67

Creating graphic arts libraries

Creation scenes

Visiting ancestors

Meeting cousins

Playing with children

Family life scenes

Checking credits balance

Visiting your vault

Looking over holdings

Investments management scenes

The little birds

What miserable worms

So long a gestation

Before they can fly

Bound to the nest

Dependant on their parents

So small a world

To roam around in

So like the birds

Spirit beings are

So long before

They are full figured

Needing delivery

Then nurturing

Until full grown

Members of society

46

The birdhouse

Winged residents

Each a great queen

Only an invisible larger

A great family

Of ripe fruits

70

Full of juice

And power

Developing and ascending

Beings throughout fatherland

With sister sky overhead

A phenomenal native

Unseen by trancers

Unknown by stupored

Family life occurred

And filled infinity

Infinity home

A great family house

To birds of a feather

Dipped in inkwells

Vastly honeycombed

Population pockets

A starship citadel

Hub and corridors

Where the heart is

You can find it

Searching deep

Beneath the surface

Space age complex

Mind machinery development

Quantum powered reality

The family tree and gallery

48

Mates for life

Psyche and symbiotic lives

Gifted by ancestral deity

To divine life

Little princes and princesses

Of the space sea realm

The invisible symbiotic beings

Occupy many minds

Home anywhere they be

Even where undesirable

Citizens of many nations

They share a court system

Two celled organisms

In complex bodies

Of perception and sensory

Multi pixel parts

Sharing control complex

Not just space

Or apparent similarities

Symbiotic bodies grow

The family of symbiotic beings

Vast establishments each

Mighty mother crafts

And great complexes

Personnel departments

Sharing identity

The body teams

And mother craft crews

The menageries' creatures

And sophisticated machinery

Identity stained in their complex

Their makers mark bearing

50

Subliminal super consciousness

Silent traveling companion

Often in the passenger seat

To conscious acts

Undesired participant

Unsought party

Unwanted guest

Often called a pest

A symbiotic being

Member of religious caste

Family of royal deities

Each with its own realm

A house of knowledge

Family bed sharing

Customarily liberal

In most policies

51

A bird can feel

A very small thing

Flying high above

Ground, trees and things

Resting on its perch

It may recollect

It is part of the flock

Growing the forest

It may reflect

Its seed generations

Swelling populations

And national complexes

Then it may recall

It is part of God's body

A co creating contributor

Not so small after all

52

Warbird's a distant cousin

Of Phoenix and firebirds

Living machines related

To birds of prey, hunting birds

Warbird is a battleship

A spacecraft designed for war

Not a pleasure craft

Or mobile home camper

Phoenix is indestructible

Rises from its ashes

It is death defiant

Will always exist

Firebird's basic transportation

Standard firepower and shields

Granting it the reputation

Of doomsday devices

The family council

Practices personal representation

Nonexclusive of representative practices

In its theater of operations

Family members can come to it

Against their family's wishes

Presenting their case or view

Before the family council

It includes every population

Developed sufficiently

To address the infinite

As a member of its intelligence

Observation towers monitor

Every part of infinity

The view well treated

To expert intelligent handling

54

Birds of a feather

Do much together

As well as look alike

And do things the same

Shows birds perform

Additionally to indulge

82

In activities of daily living

Providing much entertainment

Warbirds play games

Showing their prowess

Exercising their forces

In trial performances

The fruits of knowledge

Develop much variety

In daily access, practice, and use

Endowing life with variety

Pepper nose security

Arms limitations

Self sacrifice

For the "greater good"

Salt elimination

Defense surrendering

Martyrdom

The role models

Of fragile parties

Seeking accord

Across the board

To mortal conflicts

Just a big bomb

Eliminating any threat

Making small problems

Of any conflict scene

56

Pools support prizes

Larger than pots

In their games

Public or private

Even great game houses

Public pool purses

85

Cannot hope to match

In their biggest prizes

The marketplace too

Its market share worth

Is larger than area markets

In its profits base

Even great hosts

A vast free market

Provide for access

With their market share

Soldier, worker, star

Service provider

Activities of daily living

Experience admits

Exoteric life

Centers around these

In their combinations

Its scenes are made

Deity environment

Universal life

Nature spirits

And living things

Exoteric societies

Fail to teach, ignore

Treat nonexistent

Items of madness

58

Temple raises high

The mind and godhead

Above the din and sights

Given the average reception

The alchemists' intelligence

Or false image address

88

Seeking idol accomplice

To their chosen aims

The temple

Good posture makes

Books balanced right

On young model heads

Young deity

The average birth

The general population

In great godhead mind

The lights of heaven

Shine forth from shops

Schools and homes its light

Reveal plainly in sight

Like a candle in the window

Onlookers the light observe

Part of daily life inclusions

Even pleasant conversation

Not placed high overhead

Not spoken in secrecy

Saintly conversation

Fills daily life scenes

Except in darkened theaters

On stages with spotlights

Starring fictions performances

To the audience in plain sight

60

Knowledge of God

Fills sacred texts

And scholarly works

In heavens libraries

Not an idol's words

Or historic record

But facts of life

As God, presented

No secret made

God and life one

Sharing identity

In omnipresence

In the fiction verse

In fiction's verses

This may be heresy

Or even blasphemy

An idols carriage house

Temple complex can become

An idols horse scripture can be

An idols complex the performance

The stage may be shared

Only with itself and conscious

Subliminal and growing bodies

The two performances enacted

Family recognizes its idols

The silly Marys of the law even

With their legal complaints

About violations ongoing in life

Wanting the spotlight

A general shift in life

From family to them

Or their chosen idols

62

The light on top

Catch the wind

In their sails

Perfectly silent

Cast in webs of illusion

Or other theater scene

Light headed machines

Walk a sea of dreams

Life just beyond reception

Existing in the great din

Waiting for newcomers

With all proper receptions

In their mugs a drink

Served to enchant

Provide sleep and dreams

To carry them along

Beyond finite senses

In a place in mind

Gods and wizards

Coexist and space occupy

Beyond the mirror

Hanging on the wall

The mind is found

In which hangs all

Seeing by tables

Instead of dialog

Vision depth increases

To scientific views

Space and mind

Overlapping in thought

Two disciplines found

Of material science

64

Life by representation

A presentation to mind

An explanation for experience

Science experience confirmed

Difficult hosts make

Of foreign schools

Of alien lessons

Of new thoughts

Like a cut key

A schools view

Opening a lock

On experiences doors

A scheme guide

To experiences

The keys cut

Opening doors

Without prior knowledge

So easily taught a scheme

For life as it is known

Or that beyond experience

When the plate's been exposed

Difficult to make a clear impression

Double vision may result

Or loss of mind's grip on reality

Some schools aim to break

Student's prior logos window

For a replacement window pane

Of the schools instillation

The school of life

Contains all windows

As interpretations of life

Seen through school eyes

66

Scholar's diagrams

Far reaching guides

Prepare with references

In their instruction

The broader the view

The more scenarios equipped

100

Its students become

Facing a smaller unknown

Your choice of school

Your views will form

Thoughts conform

And life style will lead

Experience feeds

Well developed data bases

Gets received and processed

As the student was instructed

How do you do

What were you taught

Mind power and abilities

Or the constitutional matter

Can you hear a pin drop

In other dimensions

By psychic connection

Or just that in range

Can you lift mountains

At least in your mind

Or do you think in data

Instead of sensory impressions

Is space your matter

Or does it occupy space

And contain space

But can't be space

68

How much power

Can a mind generate

If a space transformer

Capable of quantum fusion

If surface matter

Tip of the iceberg

Of a space formation

Instead of foundation level

Inner space infinite

Taken at great distance

Across dimension boundaries

An inner space plane

Surface planes ice flows

Traveling through time space

Containing more space than revealed

In its surface applications

Deity power, magic

Even experience sciences

All easily explained

In infinite potentials science

Even space applied

To explaining the above

Adequate job produces

With observation and experience

As acts of a mind

The above readily explained

Instead of dismissed

As impossibilities

Only closed minds

Dismiss deity or magic

When lacking experience

Of their existence

70

A divine couple

Aspirant can become

Beside itself loving

A constant companion

Grown into awareness

Realized a potential

106

Mind and conscious

In constant company

Courtship ventured

Tokens given

Romance blooms

For conscious and mind

To not burden

Or cast a spell

Mind approached

Consciousness courter

Parked in stealth mode

Invisible to naked eyes

A space craft intelligent, living

Advanced technology can be

Partnered with its captain

Sharing a stateroom

Or occupying its own

The ship's a companion

Firepower, shield and life support

State of the art level

Standard equipment

In the symbiotic class ships

Temperaments varying

As tastes for companions

Advanced technology provides

Its privileged marketplace

72

Cook, driver, housekeeper

Nanny, bodyguard, tutor

Manager and publicist

Entourage you can be

Imager to plane entry

Physics phenomena

109

Manifestations of mind

All you need develop

A friendly audience

To your every act

You can provide

With your mind

Easy as dreaming

While fully conscious

In physics clarity

Of waking life plane

Self repairing

Self preserving

Self correcting

Higher power acts

Self defense

Self guided

Self supporting

Higher power gifts

Judgment skills

Intelligence faculty

Sane discrimination

Higher power deeds

Resident expert

Scientific genius

All knowing

Higher power titles

74

Mind, mood, behavior

Can be altered

By information chosen

For experience association

Seeing a greater good

Thinking a higher law

112

Governs everything

Can change your view

Belief in forgiveness

For most violations

For proper preparations

Changes treatment due

Expecting life without end

An eternity of living

Changes your perspective

Of the moments

Sound barriers

Block the way

To psychic reality

Nature's gifts

Thoughts can be crazy

Phenomena symptoms

Spirit friends sign of madness

Teachers all con artists

So goes public opinion

Even professionals agree

Psychic reality, spiritual life

Is not real, just make believe

Yet beyond opinions

There is knowledge

A spiritual science

Of mind and space

76

The end of ignorance

Conformity to illusion

The public presentation

Is a personal step

Choosing another window

Than usher guided to

115

For viewing experience

Can be isolating

A lonely path

Can be required

Walking upon

Changing window

Yet in the cave

The path to light

Reveals the shadows

As well as source

Window choice

Is mind expanding

Potentials revealing

Perhaps to confusion

No longer anchored

To a window view

What is left real

Not just apparent

Experience is very real

Science founded on it

Windows founded on truth

Are experience schemes

That unknown by experience

Revealed by new window

Should be able to confirm

By expanding experience

78

Beware those

Making claims

Experience a teacher

Instead of subject

Experience is illusory

How much so unknown

118

Unless deliberate deceiver

Deliberate exposure allows

Deceiver may lie concealed

Beyond observed experience

Controlling mind plane

Or space projection environments

Dismissing the very real

Potentials or possibility

Leaves you minus

Possibly the explanation

Coming home

Throwing the switch

You expect the light

Or seek an explanation

No room for doubts

Or speculations

You expect the light

Because of experience

If without prior

Experience of switch

Or light response

A different scene

Throwing switches

In a house disconnected

From power source

You'd get another view

80

Home experiences limited

Schools can teach to

Instead of teach experiences

Beyond students range

School can peg student

With stereotypes

121

Place in a character act

Resembling the student body

Life after school can be a play

An elaborate performance

Featuring the student

In a lead role act

Life can be warped

By misleading education

And subsequent on location

Performed scripted acts

How real

Life's presentation

To your experience

How much confirmed

How much

Shown to you

Instead of presented

In information vehicles

How prepared

To meet situations

By your experience

Or given education

How thorough

A representation

Of available views

In your experience

82

Who decided

What you learned

What you witness

In your experience

Who controlled

Your education

124

Was it a cross section

Of available views

Is your experience

Controlled as a set

On location performances

Presented just you

Are you the student

In a school's performance

Of scripted routine acts

Presented to just you

A logos window opened

To infinity, mind and space

I've revealed to you

Yours to choose or reject

Windows plenty

Can be opened

Customized to author

And chosen to present

Complete with fanfare

Of home and school audience

Presenting to the student

The scripted portrayal

A game show

Starring student bodies

Played on closed sets

Even on location

84

Two world views

Now before you

One mind and space

The other experience

One requires insight

Seeing beyond experience

The other is anchored

Is only what's experienced

One opens a door

Places on a path

Confirmation and living god

Claimed leading to

The other places at the door

The familiar and taught

The public viewed

Presentation of reality

Experience basis

For that held possible

In your personal view

Limits reality to experience

No place known

By mere mapmakers

Nothing shown

By science text authors

Experiences place

Is joined to truth

Like the two keys

Opening knowledge's door

Applications or texts alone

Doesn't science teach in full

Text and lab studies

Required for science degrees

86

Beyond appearances

Behind the scenes

Ancestral deity's family

Works as if unseen

Not noticed by you

Not presented to the public

130

Without great fanfare

A sacred family dwells

Whether you approach it

Make the continued effort

To breach the illusions

Between you and them

Determines the outcome

Of your hearing of god

Learning of his family

Or divine life beyond

Not ready for deity

Not ready for

Its family network

Limits your choices

You always possess

At least yourself

Much more though

May be beyond

Behind red tape

Not on the table

Even local resources

May be kept

Between worlds

Experience and knowledge

Present to you

You may have to choose

88

Underground

To establishment

Psychic reality may be

Where omitted exoteric

All the vices and virtues

Of psychic life's reality

133

May be unknown by you

In exoteric experience

Your life may be a play

Or a game being played

In exoteric experience

Behind the scenes

Fun and games

Presentable the student

Beside an education

Even in home and school

Stereotype treatment

Stereotypical handling

May be reserved for

Less than sensitive bodies

If not perfectly psychic

Or worse without perfect vision

You may be treated subject

Of a crown or realm

Enduring time spent with

Selections for of no representation

Of personal likes and dislikes

Or any personal basis

Without liberty or voice

In personal matters

As if a nonentity

Without entitlement

90

Fear the key

To understanding

The aims and goals

Of the officially dumb

Pain and insecurity

Their chosen tools

To sell their way

To their audiences

Big hairy monsters

They care to appear

To those of game disposition

To their advances

Sadists performing for sports

Their routine abuses

Of authority and power

For their fringe audience

Rogues games

In leather and lace

Lovers play

With no disgrace

Whips and chains

Used in such games

As lovers tools

Don't hurt or bind

Those playing along

Prolong the game

To its effects and sounds

Of love and loved ones

The lover dominant

Throughout the sport

Between the lovers

Playing the games

92

Tolerance straining

Some sport can be

Horseplay and leather face

Are not for everyone

An once of pain

Not for some

Whether in mind, mood

Or bodily felt

Playing to the limits

Of your endurance

Requires confidence

In sports complex

The umpire in constant

Close observation

The referee arbitrator

Of game performance

Seated in the mirrors

At the funhouse table

Of two way technology mirrors

Your image may be unrecognizable

Morphed beyond resemblance

Moving in a different direction

Your image can appear

Thanks to technology

Will you go blind

Or forget where you are

Seeing the images

Appearing so different

If it resembles another

Will you swear it so

Not you at all

But distinct, someone else

94

Positive attention

Snares faster

Than blows or bonds

Average hearts

Fringe elements

Hearts faster won

142

By blows or bonds

With relief occasions

Some elements accompaniments

Depend on for approval

Requiring insight in the deeds

For proper performance

The macabre offends

As much as entertains

Fringe elements of society

Like other acts likewise

Experience teaches its course

Reveals its mysteries to seekers

Beyond experience needs probes

Guides into the possibilities

Experience's school

May teach marvels

Its science may cure

And provide a bounty

Experience's science

Foundation may bare

Building reveal plain

Space discover within

Experience inner dimension

May expose to plain sight

Uncover resource value of

Reveal the power of applied

95

Experience in beholders eyes

Can be heaven or a hell

In the same environment

Shaped by observers perceptions

One may marvel

At advances of science

While another sees

The horrors of war craft

You can take it seriously

Or consider it theatrically

To an audience review

Perhaps even entertained

Reality is shaped by perception

Your personal view molded

Your knowledge and experiences

Forging your reactions

A shadow of a doubt

Things are as presented

Should be raised by you

If infinity is not yet probed

Doubts should rise

Things are as they appear

If mind goes undeveloped

If mind planes are not in use

Questions should be asked

If space not recognized

Vast within and about

Constitutional of matter

Realizations should be made

If science is yet exploring

Instead of finished its study

Published its findings

98

Experience a quarter the pie

Presents to its students

Inner and external space equal

Another quarter provides

Mind creation of sensory planes

Yet another fourth the pie presents

148

And the leap into infinity

Probing beyond a fourth establishes

Knowledge's pie these four contain

All views in experiences fourth

Not space equality, mind relativity

Or infinity concluding in content

In experiences appearance

Things more different than alike

More independent than joined

More vulnerable than immune

Experience the scene

Where contention lies

Where frauds sting

Where schools differ

In classrooms

The lessons absolute

Its points presented

Its conclusions drawn

However universal

Or relative to location

The lessons taught

Provide a view

A logos window

A reviewing stand

To see experience from

Every lesson provides

100

Experiences limits

Observed range of motion

Get lifted by relativity

To mind, space and infinity

Experience presents

Its fuels and power sources

151

Mind, space and infinity

Are alternative forces

Experience deceptions

A part of life to some

The given explanation

For alternative force failures

Experience expansions

Secret doctrine explanations

May be offered

In place of force substitutes

Experience is the deity

As something else

Made other out of

By an agent at work

Agencies of the mind

The ancestral deity

Transform it radically

To realms and planes

Realms are planes

Hierarchy defines a realm

Whereas planes are level

Everyone equal in it

Recreation and research

Productivity, establishment

And entertainment

Are basic agencies

102

Central heat, air, light and power

Faith can provide to you

From the living ancestral deity

You live and move within

Even around the clock security

By your big buddy body guard

The ancestral deity can provide

If you can handle the company

God can provide all your needs

Anything you desire he has

In his creations varieties

You just need get connected

Start by inviting God into you

Welcome him into your life

Let him care and provide for you

Your daily life scenes and contacts

Unless you're out of your way

To become a blot

On God within you

You have nothing to fear

God is your ancestor

May even be your Lord

He is in all existence

Even the estranged

They focus on name

Even their birthday suit

To forge their ego

Instead of on God

They identify themselves

With what God's grown

On what he's become

In his omnipresence